THE BEDSIDE BOOK
FOR VERY YOUNG GUESTS

THE BEDSIDE BOOK FOR VERY YOUNG GUESTS

Albine Taylor

The Book Guild Ltd
Sussex, England

First published in Great Britain in 2001 by
The Book Guild Ltd
25 High Street
Lewes, East Sussex
BN7 2LU

Typesetting in Souvenir Light by
IML Typographers, Birkenhead, Merseyside

Origination, printing and binding in Singapore
under the supervision of MRM Graphics Ltd, Winslow, Bucks

A catalogue record for this book is available from
The British Library

ISBN 1 85776 528 1

Contents

With a skip, a dance, a curtsy, spring has come to peep at us

6

SPRING

With a wriggle and a tickle, and twinkle in her eye,
Spring has come to peep at us from behind the
   wintry sky.

With a skip, a dance, a curtsy,
With the primrose nodding in her flurry,
She will play a game of hide-and-seek,
Bringing fresh pink tints upon our cheeks.
Then, with a laugh like tinkling bells,
Among the clouds she'll disappear again!
But never mind, she'll soon come out
To open the leaves upon the bough,
And when she settles down to stay
Our coughs and sneezes will go away!

With a wriggle and a tickle, and a twinkle in her
   eyes,
Spring has come to peep at us from behind the
   wintry sky.

A basket arrived, full of kittens, today

PIP AND SQUEAK

A basket arrived full of kitchens, today;
        All strays!
I chose one, a black and tan.
My sister took one she said was just right,
Except for some spots, it's nearly all white.
She calls it Pip
        I don't know why . . .
Mine opened its mouth, but made not a 'peep' . . .
        So I called it Squeak!

LETTY'S EARLY NIGHT

Letty Mouse brought her cup of hot chocolate up to bed with her. 'I'm tired,' she yawned as she snuggled down, 'I'll have a nice early night.'

Just then she heard a funny rattly noise on her doorstep. She sat up. Rat-a-tat-tat, rat-a-tat-tat went the knocker.

'For once I got to bed early,' she moaned, as she went down the stairs, 'and someone has to call on me!' She grumbled as she slid across the hall. 'And I have a curler in my tail!'

Rat-a-tat-tat, rat-a-tat-tat, went the knocker again.

'All right, I am coming!' she shouted as she opened the door.

'I only wanted to come and say goodnight for the winter,' said Harry Hedgehog, coming in. 'I thought it would be polite, as I won't see you until the spring.' He yawned, then seeing Letty in her dressing gown, he went on 'Oh, do you sleep all winter too?'

'No, no,' said Letty, 'I was just having an early night.'

Harry Hedgehog yawned again, and it made Letty yawn.

'This is catching,' she cried, 'Shall I make you a cup of tea to keep you awake a little longer?'

But she had not even reached the kitchen before Harry Hedgehog was fast sleep, right in the middle of her hall!

'And I have a curler in my tail'

'Dear, dear,' she cried, 'whatever shall I do? He takes up nearly all the room.' She could just squeeze past him if she was very careful, as he was so very prickly. 'Dear, dear,' she cried again, 'I cannot move him!' So she decided to go back to bed.

She was just dropping off to sleep again when she heard a soft scratchy noise on her doorstep. She sat up and listened.

'Now what can it be?' she muttered, as she put on her dressing gown.

Scratch, scratch, scratch, went the noise.

She pulled back the latch and opened the door. There, to her horror, stood Sooty the cat.

'Help!' squealed Letty as she squeezed back past Harry Hedgehog's prickles, with Sooty grinning after her.

Sooty jumped in and landed right on top of Harry Hedgehog's back!

'Meaw ... ow ... ow,' he howled as he limped out of Letty's hall. And she could still hear him going 'Meaw ... ow ... ow' as she closed the door after him. She looked lovingly at Harry.

'Good old Harry!' she panted, 'you saved my life!'

'How lucky,' she yawned, as she snuggled under her blankets, 'that Harry Hedgehog ...' she yawned again, 'fell asleep in my hall!' and she felt quite sure that at least Sooty would not call on her again that winter!

THE TORTOISE AND THE SNAKE

Lady Lucy Tortoise had lived a long time and grown very wise. But she was so slow that the animals of the wood said, 'She'll never get there!' and they went on their way.

Where was she going? Nobody knew, nor did she! But that did not worry her because she was very happy living in her own little glade. It had lots of young green grass and a spring of bubbling water.

'Hum ... Excuse me madam...' said a polite little snake. 'Can you please tell me where I am?'

Lady Lucy sunbathed in her deckchair

14

'Certainly,' replied Lady Lucy, who was sun-bathing in her deckchair; 'you are in Tortoise Glade. And you are trespassing.'

'I am what?' asked the snake.

'Trespassing!' repeated Lady Lucy. 'You know, as the notices say when people want to be private. I have pinned one on my gate.'

The snake, who could not read or write, thought Lady Lucy Tortoise very clever indeed.

'I only wanted to find the centre of these woods, but I cannot read notices!' said the snake sadly. 'I wonder if you could help me?'

Lady Lucy thought for a moment, and then she got very excited, for a wonderful idea had come into her head . . . travelling!

'Yes,' she said, 'I will come with you. It is a long time since I went away on a holiday; it will do me good, and as we are both slow we will be good company for each other.'

And they kept so busy talking, as they travelled, that they never noticed any of the other animals until they met a very hungry wolf.

'Why!' exclaimed the wolf, 'here's my supper...' and he was just going to pounce on the snake when Lady Lucy said:

'Why, Mr Wolf, I am surprised! I thought you were clever.'

'What's that?' growled the wolf. 'There's no one as clever as me in these woods ... except perhaps Mr Fox,' he added as an afterthought.

'Then,' said the tortoise, 'I'd have thought you would know better than to eat when you're puffing and panting, and far too hungry and tired, I'll be bound, to be able to digest properly. That's the way to get indigestion.'

'Indi what?' asked the wolf, surprised.

'A pain in your tummy,' explained the tortoise.

'I see...' said the wolf, who did not know many big words. 'But what can I do, because I am very hungry and have not been able to catch a thing all day!'

'I'll tell you,' said Lady Lucy Tortoise, nodding her head wisely. 'Lie down under that tree and rest. We're so slow we won't get very far ... then, when you wake up, refreshed, you'll be able to enjoy us all the more.'

Mr Wolf was very tired and rested under the tree

'That is a good idea,' cried the wolf, 'because I am very tired really.' And he started to yawn.

As soon as the wolf was snoring, Lady Lucy told the snake to climb the tree.

'But what are you going to do?' asked the snake.

'I'll lock myself up in my house.'

'But,' whispered the snake, who had reached the lowest branch, 'you are a long way away from home!'

'Ssh . . . don't argue! Do as I say and you will see.'

When the wolf woke up, he found, to his surprise, no snake and no tortoise by his side.

'But,' he thought to himself, 'they are so slow, they could not possibly get very far!' He fumbled in his pocket and muttered: 'Where are my glasses?'

Even with his glasses on he could see nothing but a big shell. He poked it and pushed it, but there was nothing underneath it. It was shell all the way round. The little snake thought this very funny, and laughed. The wolf looked up.

'Aha!' he yelled hungrily, 'I still have you!' and he started to climb the tree. But he was not very good at climbing trees. So he tried to jump, but when he tried to jump from the first to the second branch, it cracked ... and he tumbled to the ground with a terrible CRASH! He tore his fur, cut his paw, broke his glasses, and ran all the way home to nurse his bruises.

As soon as he was gone, Lady Lucy Tortoise came out of her shell and the snake came down the tree.

'Let's go home to Tortoise Glade,' sighed Lady Lucy. 'This outside world is wearing me out!'

The little snake, who had just had a very lucky escape, agreed. And they never stopped on their way home until they reached the gates of Tortoise Glade.

'PRIVATE PROPERTY.

TRESPASSERS WILL BE PROSECUTED,'

read Lady Lucy, as she unlocked the gate. And there they lived, happily, and much more safely, for a very long time.

In the heather I lie dozing, with the bumble-bee droning

SUMMER

In the heather, I lie dozing
With the bumble-bee droning,
And the rustle of the leaves
Of the rich green trees
Talks to me of many dreams.
I tell the trees' dreams.
To the fleeting white clouds
Who puff them over the world around.
But I lie, here, dozing . . .
With the bumble-bee droning . . .
The summer's hot sun for blanket,
Not wishing to awaken just yet!

Bonzo and Bruno went for a walk in the woods

A WALK IN THE WOODS

For the first time in their lives, the two little bears, Bonzo and Bruno, came to live in the country. One sunny day they went for a walk in the woods at the bottom of their lane. As they went along the path they heard a buzzing sort of noise: buzz buzz ... zzzz. It seemed to be coming nearer, and suddenly they saw a small fat insect wearing a brightly striped jumper in black and yellow.

'Excuse me,' started Bonzo, very politely, 'but could you please tell us what you are?'

Mrs Bee buzzily collected nectar from the flowers

'Buzzz . . . yesssss . . . I am a buzy buzzing bee.'

'Oh!' said Bonzo and Bruno together, 'a bee! And could you tell us what you are doing?'

'Yessss, I am collecting nectar from the flowers. Buzzzz . . .'

'Nectar?' asked the bear puzzled. 'Why?'

'To make honey, of course.'

'It must be wonderful to be able to make your own honey!' exclaimed the bears. 'We love honey!' But they quickly remembered their manners and added, 'Thank you, Mrs Bee.'

They saw something disappearing down a hole

Suddenly they saw something flash past them and disappear down a hole. They peered inside, but it was too dark to see anything.

'And what do you think you are doing, peering down my front hall?' demanded a tiny voice from behind them.

'Sorry,' replied the bears, turning round slowly to face a furry animal with long ears and a twitchy nose. 'But we saw something disappear down that hole. Do you know what it was?'

'Yes, of course. It was me.'

Bonzo and Bruno were filled with curiosity. 'What were you doing down there?' they asked.

'I live down there,' answered the rabbit, twitching his nose.

'In a hole?' The bears just could not believe this.

'Of course,' retorted the rabbit impatiently, 'All rabbits do, you know, except those who live in hutches. . . . But then they are not really proper rabbits; they are pets!' He scratched his ear, then added, 'If you'll excuse me now, I have a lot to do. You see, we have only just moved in today, and my wife wants everything to be ready before nightfall.'

The bears just saw the white bob of his tail disappear down the hole and they shouted after him, 'Goodbye!'

A little further on they heard a tap, tap, tapping. They looked around but could see no one. Tap . . . tap . . . tap . . .

'That is funny,' said Bruno, 'I am sure I heard someone tapping at somebody's door. But I cannot see anyone.'

'I cannot even see a house,' agreed Bonzo. Then he saw a bird in a tree, so he went and asked him very politely, 'Excuse me, but did you hear a knocking?'

'Yes, it was me,' answered the brightly-coloured bird as he tapped on the tree trunk.

'Is there somebody living in that tree, then?' asked Bonzo.

'I can't see the door,' added Bruno.

'There are lots of insects living just under the bark of the tree,' said the bird. 'When I tap, it disturbs them and then I catch them as they come out. That is how I get my dinner.'

'I never knew birds did that! I thought they fed on seeds,' said the little bears, in amazement.

'Ah!' laughed the bird, 'No, no, my friends, I do it because I am a woodpecker.'

'Well, thank you, Mr Woodpecker, for telling us,' said the bears, and they went on their way, leaving the woodpecker to get his dinner.

By now they were tired and they sat on an old tree trunk for a rest. But suddenly, out popped a sharp-faced animal with a lovely bushy tail and very pointed ears. In its paws it held a nut, and with its sharp little front teeth it nibbled at it. It winked at the bears, and said, 'Like a nut?'

'Have you got many stored in this hollow tree trunk?' they asked.

'Yes, this is my store. I hide them here in the autumn so that I can find them when I wake up in the spring.'

'Do you mean you sleep all winter?' asked Bonzo, in surprise.

'Well, most of the time. Not all the time, but most of the time ... All squirrels who respect themselves do!' answered the squirrel in a very superior sort of way. 'So do hedgehogs. Look, there is one coming now.' He pointed to a walking pincushion, but when the bears went near him to shake paws, he curled up into a tight ball, and that was the end of that.

Soon the bears were on their way again, and in a glade full of bluebells, they picked so many flowers that their arms nearly ached with the weight.

'Look, there is a dog!' cried Bruno, pleased to see one animal he could recognise.

'But doesn't he smell horrid!' said Bonzo, as the dog came nearer.

'I'm looking for a nice fat rabbit for supper. Have you seen any lately?' asked the dog.

'Goodness! You must be the fox!' cried the bears in terror. 'No wonder the rabbits live down holes; it is safer!'

They ran as fast as their fat little legs could carry them, past the squirrel who had finished chewing his nuts, almost falling over the hedgehog who was still curled up in a ball; past where the woodpecker tapped away at the tree trunk, and on to where the rabbits had just finished their new home.

'Hurry! Hurry!' they cried, breathless from their long run. 'Mr Fox is on his way.'

'Thanks for the warning!' cried the rabbits, as they flashed home, and only their little bobbing white tails could be seen for a moment before the bears were once again on their way. They walked on, their arms full of flowers, when they met Mrs Bee once again, who was still buzzily gathering nectar.

'That was kind of you to warn the rabbit family,' she said buzzzingly. 'In the country we always help one another. Now here is a little treat for your tea.' And she gave them some nice sweet honey.

When they got home the little bears cried excitedly, 'Look, Mummy! Flowers for you and some honey for tea!'

A few minutes later they all sat down to a delicious tea. There were bluebells in a vase in the middle of the table, and lovely toasted teacakes thickly coated with honey!

They took a long time over tea that day, because they had so much to tell their mother.

'It is wonderful living in the country!' they both agreed. 'There are so many nice people to meet, and so many nice things to see, and so many exciting things to do.'

In a way they even felt sorry for Mr Fox, and hoped he had found something for his supper, without having to hurt the rabbits.

They slept very well that night, and every other night, so that they could be up early in the morning and go out to meet all their new friends, for another nice long day of adventure.

In the autumn moonbeams, jewelled ghosts to me they seem

AUTUMN

The magic of the autumn hues,
The reds, the golds, the mauves, the blues
Display their galaxy of shades
And spread them at our feet to fete.
They swirl, and toss, and crackle crisply
Rustling in a frenzied dancing.
The reds, the golds, the mauves, the blues
Dance through the night, covered in dew,
And in the autumn moonbeam
Jewelled ghosts, to me, they seem.
But through the days, to lengthening shadows
The colours blend, splash, mix and mellow
All joining in a carnival feast
As if in a last attempt to please.
The reds, the golds, the mauves, the blues,
To the autumn magic, pay their dues.

Bimbo ran his fingers along the bars of the door

BIMBO AND THE TREE
HE COULDN'T CLIMB

Bimbo was having a nice game of hide-and-seek with the zookeeper. Bimbo was the bright spot of the zoo, because he was a very funny little monkey. The keeper turned away to clean out the cage.

'Aha,' thought Bimbo, 'the door is open! and he ran his fingers along the bars. Suddenly the door opened wide, and Bimbo ran out. 'Ugh! Ugh!' cried Bimbo in delight, as he jumped into a tree.

What a wonderful time he had swinging from tree to tree! He gurgled happily, 'Ugh, ugh, ugh,' and then he swung out of a big tree and flopped onto the lawn to do some somersaults. He lay tired and happy in the shade of a very big tree.

'Ugh! Ugh! he cried, looking up. 'There is a tree I really *must* climb,' and he shot up, making a very big leap. But when he reached the lowest branch he cried out in pain, 'Oh!' and then he tried again, but once more he cried 'Oh!' and fell down. Again and again he tried, but each time he fell down, crying 'Oh ... Oh ...' This was very painful! At last he gave up trying to climb that tree, and he flopped to the ground with a very big flop, and stayed there feeling very tired indeed.

By now the keeper had finished cleaning out the monkey house, and just to make quite sure everything was all right, he counted all the monkeys.

'One ... two ... three ... four ... five.' He stopped and scratched his head, then he started again. 'One ... two ... three ... that's funny,' he said all at once, 'I can't see Bimbo ... Now where can he be hiding? He loves his game of hide-and-seek!'

But no matter how hard he called and looked, he just could not find Bimbo. The keeper got very worried, and decided to go to the SUPER-INTENDENT'S house to tell him Bimbo was lost.

'Oh!' said the keeper, as he walked across the lawn, 'I wonder what that is lying under that tree?' and he walked to where Bimbo lay. 'Why, it's Bimbo!' He picked up the tired little monkey.

'Ugh ... Ugh ... Ugh,' whimpered Bimbo, looking up at the tree.

'You silly little monkey!' laughed the keeper, 'You can't climb that tree. It's a MONKEY-PUZZLE!' And he was still laughing as he put Bimbo back into his cage, making quite sure this time that the door was properly shut.

But Bimbo didn't mind; he was glad to be back and find his cosy little bed. And there he stayed, all afternoon, curled up and fast asleep. And all the children thought he was just as funny as before, with only his nose peeping over his sheet, and his long tail hanging over the foot of his bed.

And there he stayed curled up and fast asleep

Winter snows make you glad to be at home

WINTER SNOWS

Sledges gliding down the hill,
Winds that whistle cold and chill,
Ears and noses blue with cold,
Fingers which refuse to hold.

Snowmen standing fat and big
Whilst we dance round in a jig.
Icicles dripping from the twigs
Of trees that wear great snowy wigs.
Skies, heavy, dark and grey,
Promising more snow on the way.

But with curtains drawn after dark,
And teacakes toasting by the hearth,
The winter snows, and fires that glow
Make you glad to be at home!

'Look down at your feet, dear, the moon lies in the water'

THE PUDDLE

'Mother dear, mother dear, I want the moon.
Please, mother dear, will you give it me soon?'

'If you want the moon, my sweet little daughter,
Look down at your feet, it lies there in the water.'

'But I want the one which shines brightly,
The one in the sky, the one which looks mighty!'

'Look down at your feet, dear, look into that puddle
And see how the Mighty One shines when lowly and
    humble.'

'The moon at my feet! So close to me?
I'll bend down and take it, wait and see!'

'You'll shatter your dream, dear, if you breathe on
    that water,
For here, at your feet, lies the truth, my dear daughter.
The honest share with that puddle a perfect dream,
But it becomes a nightmare when you try to be
    greedy and mean!'

On top of Sally's shelf sat a very handsome Teddy

THE RAINBOW TEDDY

On top of Sally's nursery shelf sat a handsome white nylon Teddy. When she had friends in to tea, she told them: 'Granny gave me that lovely Teddy for Christmas. He is my very best toy. Mummy says I must look after him, so we had better not play with him, because white shows the dirt so.'

Teddy felt sad because he longed to be played with, and he wished he were an old toy.

One night he climbed down from his shelf, and had a good look round the nursery. On the shelf, just below his, he found Sally's paints and brushes, and a jar of very dirty water. Suddenly he longed to paint a picture . . . of himself. So he sat down on the rug, and dipped a brush in the dirty water, then stirred it in the paints, round and round, just as he had seen Sally do that afternoon. He painted a picture of himself, but it was a brown teddy . . .

'I wish I were brown – brown doesn't show the dirt'

'I wish I were brown!' he sighed, 'brown doesn't show the dirt so much!' He growled as he cleaned the brush, but he only made the water even dirtier. He looked at the jar and thought, 'It looks like honey. I wonder what it tastes like?' He put the tip of his nose into the jar, because he loved honey, and wished he could have some. But it did not taste like honey at all! It was horrid!

He coughed and spluttered and made funny faces ... then spilled the dirty water all down his lovely white nylon fur front! He dropped the jar in his fright, and spilled the rest of the dirty water all over the paintbox, making a terrible mess.

He tried hard to tidy up, but could not quite reach the shelf, so that the paintbox fell upside down on top of his lovely white nylon fur head, leaving little spots of paint all over it! Poor Teddy! He sobbed himself to sleep, just where he was, right in the middle of the rug. And when he woke up, he heard someone else sobbing. It was Sally.

Poor Teddy was all the colours of the rainbow

'My poor Teddy! she sobbed. 'You have all the colours of the rainbow on your forehead!'

'It certainly looks like it. I think he must have fallen head first in the paint box,' agreed her mother.

'I wish now that I had tidied up last night before going to bed ... then this would not have happened!' said Sally.

She picked him up and cuddled him, and Teddy felt very sorry for her.

'I will call you my Rainbow Teddy!' cried Sally, cheering up suddenly. 'And now I can play with you any time I like!'

How the children laughed when they saw him, but Teddy didn't mind. He was no longer lonely, and he had a secret! He had not *fallen* from the shelf, had he?